A Private View

by
Ruchi Kohli

PublishAmerica
Baltimore

First printing

ISBN: 1-4137-9077-1
PUBLISHED BY PUBLISHAMERICA, LLLP
www.publishamerica.com
Baltimore

Printed in the United States of America

Dedication:

In loving memory of
Professor G.L. Setya
and also Dr. Wayne Dyer, Ms. Arati Kohli, Ms. Shanna
Young, Sheru Singh.

Acknowledgements:

I would like to thank Mr. Chuck Allen for his photography that appears on the front and on the back cover. I also would like to thank Ms. Sandra R. Bluett for her drawings and for her assistance with manuscript preparation.

Introduction:

A collection of poems and illustrations that invoke one's imagination to draw our own lines of thought. Our mind is like a canvas that holds colors of thought painted by experience and emotion. These vivid arrays of feelings are expressed by words and pictures to shape our reality. The design of our art in its play with size, shapes, style, tone, and intensity is challenged by space and time. Its creativity is defined from the boundaries established through conditioning whether traditional or cultural beliefs which develop into our frame of reference. The stroke of one's brush determines the fate of its projection. The mark of one thought determines its reality captured by space and time. Perception varies depending on the focus of our view as awareness to see is defined from moment to moment, space to space, beginning and ending at a point. This point of view then defines our position freeing us to travel beyond the limitations of one's mind allowing only the heart to enter this sacred ground. It is in this ground where reality enters new dimensions leading us to the essence of real. This inner cultivation of character can lead to an outer resonance as the outside world is only known in relation to the inner point of view. Hold that brush to remove the barrier of subjectivity that prevents you from realizing your essential oneness with all things. Experience this work to draw your own picture held as your Private View.

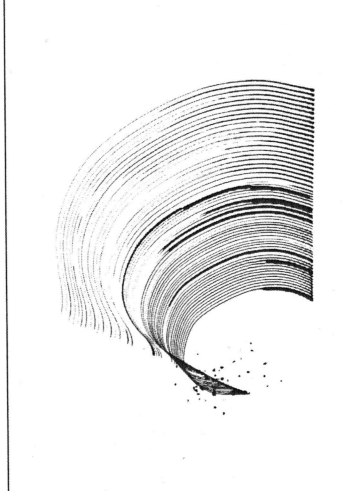

Sightseeing

With a world full of sights, what will you see?
What is the depth with which you view?
Where do you roam to find this scene?
Taking breath far away, killing even time.
Visions that are clear are blurred by sight.
Beauty you seek is framed within.
Awareness of an artist as these sights are unseen.
Perception of form eye envisions alone.
Bringing focus to view its depth to heart.
Sensitive with feel puts observe on notice.
Caressing that tear whose sorrow ran deep.
Quenching its thirst as it longs to live.
Whispers of air that measure this pulse,
Speak with silence as it died to be heard.
What sight do you seek looking back at you?
Reaching this point makes world out of sight.
Become the Sight, the World comes to view.

Desperate

I want to see you when you look for me.
Caught eye to eye with nowhere to escape.
Seeking to find are eyes that see.
Together this vision we hold of Us.
Clutching this sight as dreams do bring.
A caress of a whisper who held this secret.
As love resides in every pulse of mine.
To carry a beat that's racing with air.
Running with speed to catch this breath.
Before this time takes it away.

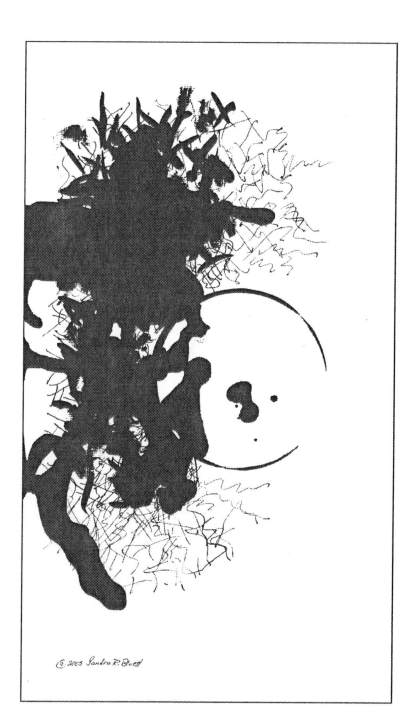

© 2005 Sandra R. Bluett

Him

Caught by this air with nowhere to escape.
Sound a mystery what his words would say.
Gasping this breath was attentive to note.
Prolonging each moment was desperation to hear.
Too shy to speak what heart always felt.
Beating each breath were pulses of him.

Worth Remembering

Moments create impressions, embossed to last.
Flavored by feelings, forever with life.
Dated with numbers, remembered as time.
Youth was exhausted just waiting to arrive.
Anticipating a play worth remembering each day.
Love being featured, spellbound by breath.
Breath went away, exhausted with sigh.
Moment to remember for what it's worth.

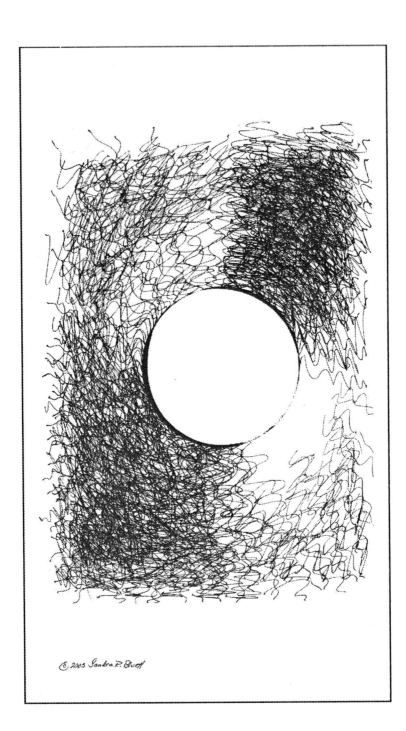

© 2003 Sandra P. Bluett

Silence

Silence knows all by hearing what's real.
Talking with depth uttering no word.
Deep with layers giving time its space.
Stilled by a moment as time can tell.
Silence only speaks to those who listen.
As making time to listen spaces silence to form.

(Silence is the only voice of God.)

A Time to Stand

Life a candle flickering with sight.
Illumines a vision who seeks a form.
Searching to find its illusions of real.
Tears hold cry framing their sorrow.
While happiness is collected dropping its tears.
Attention must pay for happiness to stay.
Time must stand to sit down and pray.
Time never stands as a clock on a wall.
Shifted by seconds as running for time.
Silence must notice this depth to view.
Awareness to see stilled as a period.
This dot of eye crossing each tee.
Wake up before this date arrives.
Remembrance of life stood up by time.

Life

Life is a script dated by time.
Who's the author writing each line?
Notice the view you dare not see.
As this is life looking back at you.
Time moves on as it marches every hour.
Looking at a mirror were reflections of Self.
The You and the Me we really can't see.
Forever will wait this date with time.
Someday to view this Life as I.

Beauty

Truth in beauty is not easy to find.
Eyes are deceptive as they seek outside.
Blinded by a sight who envisions a queen.
Design an art that never fades with time.
Create a portrait that's framed in love
Hung in a gallery that's not limited to view.
With a depth to view can only be seen.
By an eye's awareness to sights unseen.
Real Beauty can only be perceived,
By minds enlightened, far sighted from view.

Empty

Empty allows space its freedom.
Space binds freedom to thought.
Freedom limits thought with time.
Thought restricts time with view.
Time to view perceived with empty.
Perception with Empty makes life full.

Positivity

Energy will flow budding one to grow.
Seeded in Divine is the creative line.
Cultivate the tree pruning it in me.
Come rain or shine, I strive each time.
I try my best as my strength is tested.
Solid with care grounding my Earth.
Each seed of thought grows into deed.
As branches of pride were cut from this trunk.
Tough is its nature which forces this change.
Grown as a tree of life for me.

Justify

It is the nature of law to justify our means.
Judged by a thought as ruled by the mind.
Perception is limited as bounded by time.
Framed only by reference restricted by space.
Dimension to view is barred to the intellect.
Intangible by thought to justify it not.

(Almighty is perceived in dimensions not permitted to the conscious
mind where judgment resides.)

Freedom of Speech

If thoughts were free captured only in speech,
What language would tell inaudible by word.
A cry so loud that no one could hear.
A pain in the heart held only by tear.
A wound in feel bandaged only by grief.
A gaze that penetrates its desperation with fear.
A touch of a feel caressed only by wind.
A pulse of the air sensed only by breath.
This was the freedom not allowed to speech.

Wisdom

Wisdom isn't connected with life nor age.
Its essence a mystery until it arrives.
Accompanied with enlightenment broadens its view.
Related to knowledge with experience to some.
Silence its language spoken by few.
Attached to none with truth to word.
This was the wisdom meant to be heard.

Illusion

Wind breaks its flight current by current.
Mind changes direction one thought at a time.
Even silence breaks its language word by word.
An ocean is created one drop at a time.
As fragrance of breeze carries its aroma.
To fill up a space who teases this air.
Holding me hostage was this breath of time.
Creating a reality was this illusion of mine.

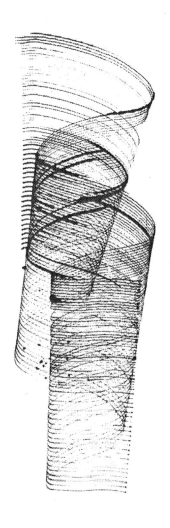

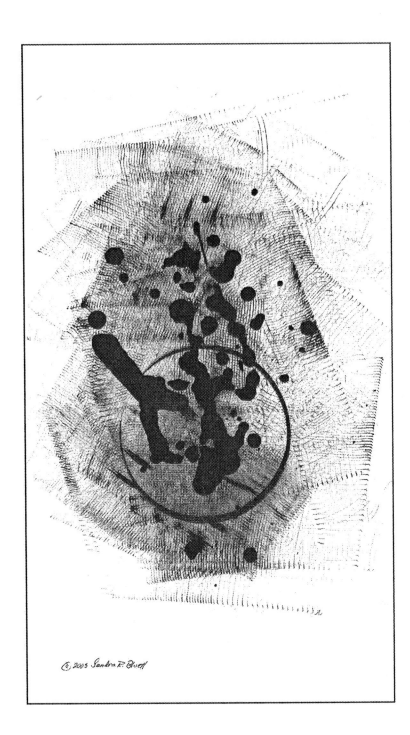

© 2003 Sandra R. Bluett

Look

Looks are what sell in the market today.
Ornaments that shine can't deceive this time.
Bold and courageous like a thief in the night.
Collection of cars makes image just right.
Degrees and trophies frame me as all.
Slender and fit show me as chic.
This was the look sold out as "Style".

Look at the Me you really don't see.
Truth that speaks without a word.
Respect that wears without collars of pride.
Fashion with flare showing I care.
A touch that can feel sensed only by love.
Language can't describe this feature as style.
As this was the look only beauty had owned.

Service

Tied with labor in deed with Love.
Look at sights no one wishes to see.
Listen to sounds no one wants to hear.
Feel the pain who expresses its presence.
Touch the feel no one cares to know.
Know all this, Self comes into view.
Live all this, of Service are You.

Imagination

Thoughts are free to run wild and be.
Wonders not restricted with space nor time.
Drama with color projects sights with sound.
Captured by a dream where characters come alive.
Soft cuddly rabbit invited by snow.
While music made silence symphony of sound.
Nature made bunny come out to play.
Twitching its nose as if to wish,
Why can't this world just let me exist!

Love

Am I in love or is love in Me?
Love is to give without receiving.
Love is to Be without changing.
Love is to hold without squeezing.
Love is to unveil without disguising.
Love is freedom barred not by thought.
Love is forever, how long does this last?
Love is with depth with shallow to view.
Love is a breath released by air.
Love is a connection without a tie.
Love is a feel without a touch.
Love is the You being in Me.

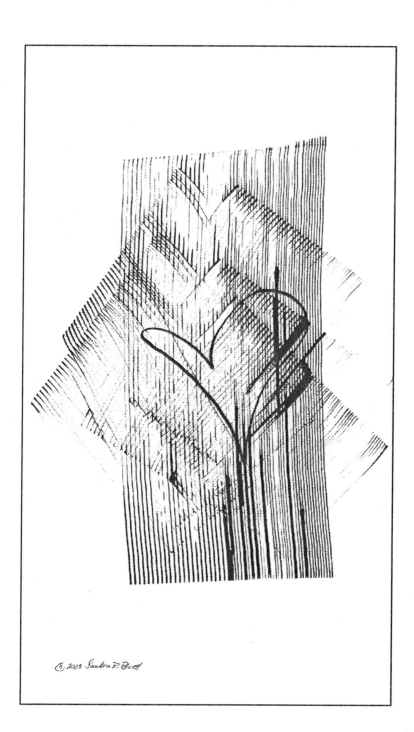

Prayer

Thank you for peace you gave me today.
The bread I eat you made for me.
The home I reside with comfort and care.
The eyes that can see beauty that's real.
The effort I keep to do no harm,
In thought, word and deed, with silence I speak.
The family you gave to support this life.
The air that I breathe till I go home.
Oh Spirit, do hear what my heart can tell.
For words can't capture my gratitude too well.

Answer

She speaks with silence inaudible to most.
Intense is her voice with passion I hear.
Languaged in truth as lived by her word.
Stilled was this gap who takes in this view.
These pockets of air hold prayers to be.
Receiving her message allows connection within.
Charged for her time were moments that passed.
To release my space who answered her call.

(Answer her call by living her message. It is heard in pin drop silence!)

Last Call

Listen to sound that's dying to be heard.
Its voice is mute as her last call is made.
With silence she speaks ringing with fear.
Dialing each number dated by time.
Blocking this call could cost her her life.
Desperate with plea to let her be free.
These words carry messages held only in prayer.
Essence of prayer answered only by heart.

Prayer

I pray for the one whose eyes have seen fear.
I pray for this pain for its healing to begin.
I pray for the animal whose soul isn't recognized.
I pray for the ignorant for God to grant her wisdom.
I pray for the swift to lead by following.
I pray for the aggressor to gain strength in character.
I pray for the bold to be soft with silence.
I pray for the poor to grant abundance in mind.
I pray for this silence as it longs to be heard.
I pray for this hunger for its starvation to end.
I pray for this empty to be full in thought.
I pray for this world to unite in peace.
I pray for the blind who witness much.
I pray for the handicapped who challenge us.
I pray for this faith to grow strong with love.
I pray most of all for the soul whose spirit has left them.
May the Almighty grant her precious grace upon all.

Beautiful

Truth to beauty is not easy to find.
Eyes are blind when they focus outside.
Search this truth that dwells within.
Focus with view brings depth to see
That beauty's not visible to this naked eye.
Even photos can't capture this image with lens.
As reflections of beauty reside in a space.
Covering her face with her hands of Love.

Day Dreams

Fantasy carries dream far from sleep.
Waking up reality forever to see.
That pulse in the air measures your breath.
Counting every moment racing every beat.
Wake up this reality as its time is short.
Dreaming of days with nights that sleep.

(Wake up this illusion called Life. Shift awareness from the experiencer, to observer, to becoming co-creator.)

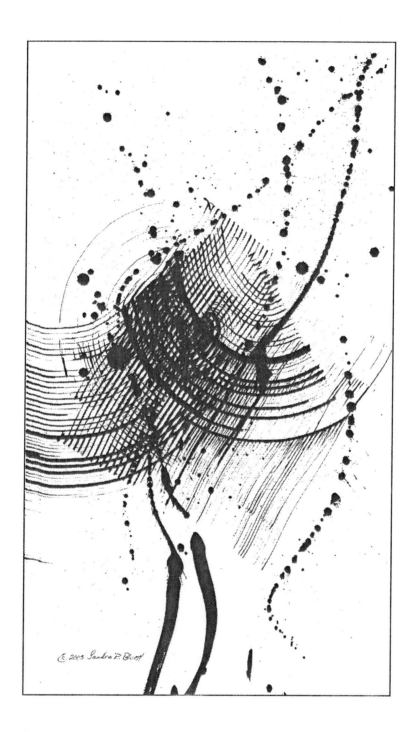

© 2003 Sandra P. Blewett

Prayer

Grant me the wisdom to see beyond sense.
To view without judgment of light from this dark.
Engage actions that love directing my words.
Grant me a hand that heals every pain.
Carry a voice that soothes even tear.
Patience with time as forever I wait.
Listening to silence as it carries your voice.
Channel my cravings for starving within.
Immerse thoughts of you for mind to be free.
Gathering my breath to merge it with you.

(Ego dies as Self emerges.)

Youth

Hung up this youth as it had worn out inside.
Tattered by time as its size didn't fit.
Image will project this feel on its face.
Screaming at thoughts for its life to begin.
Be gentle each moment caressing this wind.
Filling this empty with a vessel that's full.
As each sigh of air whispers to breath.
Immerse in this silence as treasure I have sent.
Youth is forever, not measured by time.

(Forever Young!)

Inaudible

Music is life with rhythm to beat.
Singing with laughter dancing each step.
Listening to silence that's symphony of sound.
Strumming this wind as it dies to hear.
Conversing with notes gathered air to sigh.
Gasping for breath as he clings for more.
Crying with silence who was deaf to most.
Voice went mute as it died to be heard.

(Listen to animals who become victims of our hunt and tests. Their
silence breaks my heart.)

Mummy

If love could see its image with eye,
Reflection of her saw eyes that dream.
Eye would be jealous being restricted to form.
Heart being allowed being sacred in space.
She caressed my tear with sorrow to fall.
Wiping this fear when time stood still.
Moving my clock that to forgot to tick.
Waiting with time giving space to form.
Balancing my mind with a heart that knows.
Laughter with sound while sorrow arrived.
She is my mother whose beauty will stay.
Forever in dreams till eyes go blind.

Told

Silence will hear never to tell.
View this depth these sights unseen.
Forming to appear were thoughts that observe.
Witnessed by much as thoughts do count.
Projecting a life forces tears to fall.
Dropping its sorrow as silence had broke.

Comfort

Hugging a form that's cozy and warm.
Soothing its fear who's afraid no more.
Worn like a shoe that fits just right.
Dancing each step to notes that lead.
Singing were tunes who direct me forward.
Marching to a time who lifts every moment.
Waiting to become can't come too soon.
As you have arrived, not a minute too late.

Voice

Listen to sound without a word.
Straight is its tongue which action can see.
Invisible it is as air to breath.
Carrying a silence heavy to weight.
Words can't capture this inaudible to form.
As it storms at this wind without deference to speech.
Reaching this scale makes language unheard.
Answer its call by actions that speak.
A voice that's heard without using a word.

© 2003 Sandra P. Booth

Religion

Religion divides this world from one.
Separating its spirit as a body with a hole.
Wake up this sleep so one can rest.
Observing this witness who's chained to a thought.
Viewing this mind who's intoxicated by time.
Bringing a pleasure were fruits that delight.
Plant your seed with thoughts of care.
Bow to a light who shares its warmth.
If sun doesn't care who's black from white,
And water moves forward conforming to space,
Why must this thought of religion divide?

(God has no religion. God is love.)

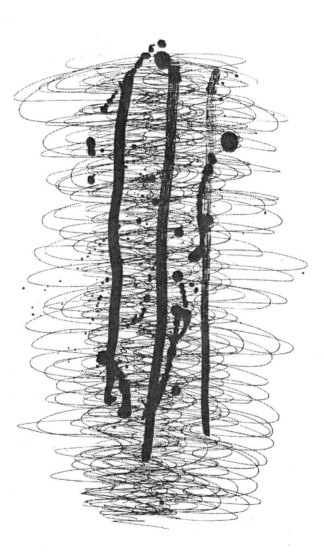

Hide and Seek

Hiding a scar difficult to face.
Marking its color was red who bleeds.
Seeking a silence that's far from view.
Waiting for time to heal this form.
Looking outside to find what's missing.
Stimulates a world with a power to look.
Hiding this world was this vision of mine.

Truth

I write to father who watches my moments.
Moment that's spent in thoughts that play.
Play who gathers ice creams and fun.
Seeking no silence for notes to breathe.
Holding no space as its home is full.
Wisdom only comes when ego is emptied.
Desire to seek to know this view.
Revealing this mystery is truth who lives.
Becoming a vision for all to see.
Live this NOW as thoughts now know.
This is the moment when truth is free.

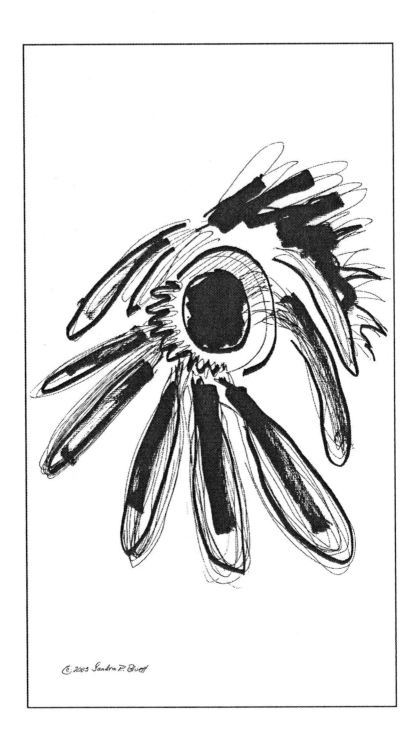

© 2003 Sandra P. Bluett

Tears

If shedding of tears could bring back his form,
An ocean couldn't hold these drops of sorrow.
Playing with time who didn't play fair.
Arriving each moment, never missing a beat.
Taking his breath stolen by air.
Time couldn't catch these chains that connect.
Tied by a moment who arrived too fast.
Running to release its attachment to form.
Dropping to knees was relief of Cry.

Old Age

When did this youth arrive as worn?
Tattered by time with worry to hide.
Gracing each year were lines on the face.
Powder can't mask this mystery inside.
As eyes view a shadow who figures it all.
Age is eternal not seen by I.

Snow

Imagine a flake falling as snow.
Covering its nature as it sits on the ground.
Waiting for time for making it move.
Fighting with air that shapes it to form.
Chill is its feel as it warmed up to drop.
Dry are its limbs as powdered with dust.
Light as this wind who pockets this air.
Caressing each whisper with a current unknown.

(Future—who knows?)

Time

Time didn't hold us together with form.
Gripping with fight was exhausted this air.
Light breaks up this hour from sleep.
Awakening a mystery who arrives on time.
To show us a view which takes our breath.
Distance must travel to witness this scene.
Bringing focus to see this experience as "Me".

(I am formless!)

Farewell

Farewell my friend as I bid you so long.
Passing this time were speedy and fast.
Forever I thought was time on your side.
With a life that was full gathered by love.
These tears that I shed are drowning in sorrow.
As I miss you so much grief stricken in pain.
Realizing that tomorrow we will meet you again.
Standing with time who waits for the hour.
To bring us together eternal with time.

(His soul lives forever, not limited by time.)

Love

I never did tell you that I love you.
I never did say for your ears to hear.
I never did write so you could look to see.
I never show you with a touch or a feel.
I never did sing a love song for you.
I never did whisper these secrets to you.
They travel in packages not visible to eye.
Delivered by grace who carries it away.
Revealing its depth to a feel who touches.
Who listens to silence not uttering a word.
Defined as forever for hours do speak.
Arriving at love who defines its own form.

(Love breaks all boundaries of space and time.)

Time

I peek out of my window of time to see.
To look out to find his form once more.
Why does this carriage only move forward?
Reversing no option as it leaves me behind.
It forms a space, invisible with depth.
Observing each count holding my breath.
I peek out this window of time to see.
Brighter a view as I look up ahead.
Papa seen smiling as dreams come true.
Waiting for time to open my door.

Sound

If sound could be captured in an image of frame.
Defining its Self for our eyes to view.
Imagine what it looked like to a touch or a feel.
Flexible with bend as it follows with sway.
A ship that can coast rough notes to safety.
A bird that can lift this loud to calm.
Carrying its tune as fragrance of breeze.
Notes only follow this symphony as sound,
When silence awakens depth to beats of a heart.

(Ego Dies as Self Emerges.)

© 2005 Sandra R. Bloett

Insight

Finally this time made moment arrive.
Arriving with wisdom for clear is its view.
Sharp its image as vision does see.
Observing a form that was missing in thought.
Sight is visible with eyes that are shut.
Held by a silence who reads each thought.
Illumining each thought that's come to play.
Calm its nature as one observes.
Intense with layers as time does show.
That pebble in the sand with dust its color.
That breeze in the air with cool its feel.
That note that is held by a space who hears.
Praying to spirit who awakens my sleep.
Giving me peace who has come to stay.
Soothing my mind who's enlightened and calm.
Arriving with love making life a dream.

(Insight brings vision to see that life of spirit begins and ends with love.)

Song

Sing with joy who is happy with sound.
Carry a tune that is full of life.
Birds tweet songs flying with color.
To travel in melody with notes of thrill.
Elephants also trumpet, their trucks in defiance.
Stomping each step, rocking with roll.
Horses hold gallop, trotting with sway.
Marching to a tone that's smooth like jazz.
Soft little bunny invited this show.
Hopped to the front leading this race.
Piggies and cows had rhythm with blues.
As they were the ones people thought of as food.
Writing this song with lyrics that feel.
Erasing each word that's noted with cry.
Carry a tune that's gentle to nature.
Tasting each line, not bitter on tongue.
Illusive its spirit, our world of song.
Together let's sing this verse as One.

(Uni-Verse—One song. Animals have a voice inaudible to us creating
a tune that's symphony of sound—love.)

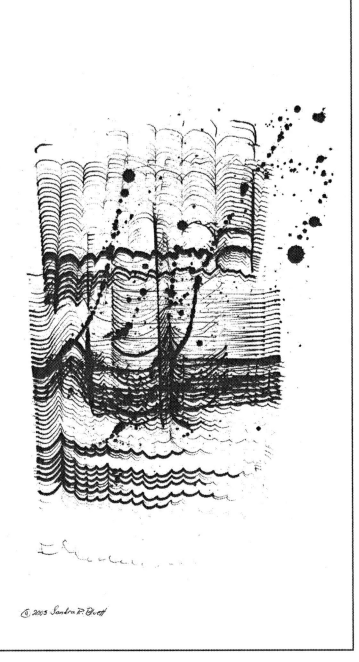

© 2005 Sandra R. Bluett

Life

Walking with time who records every minute.
I thought I could forget these hours of sleep.
Resting were thoughts who observed it forever.
Life only comes with seconds of time.
Eternal to form as spirit now sees.
Jolted was breath who gives it a life.

Wake up this moment for its time is short.
Instant its life as death has arrived.
To display a reality with an essence of real.
Showing was wisdom as simple as a leaf.
Who gathered its wind carrying it away.
Leaving its mark was fragrance of breeze.

(Seeded with grace this life of mine.)

Birthday Prayer

Forgive me Spirit as I am reminded once more.
This abundance you gave to support my life.
A mind that holds thoughts of positive.
Speech that carries tunes of cheer.
Strong is my will as defined by You.
With wisdom to see beyond all this.
Waiting a skill I still must develop.
As perfect your vision which eyes the Self.
Grant me this patience to wait for my time.
As precious each hour that is spent with You.

Us

What you thought was yours, will once be gone.
What were once your thoughts, will no longer be.
What was yours to hold, will change in time.
What was yours to touch, will feel no more.
What mattered the most, will come to an end.
When this show is over, you will begin to see.
This form thought yours, was always US.
Why must this breath be carried away,
For its life to see its was always US?

Printed in the United States
42686LVS00014BA/184

9 781413 790771